Brando
Rides
Alone

Other Books by Barry Gifford

Fiction
Do the Blind Dream?
American Falls: The Collected Short Stories
Wyoming
My Last Martini
The Sinaloa Story
Baby Cat-Face
Arise and Walk
Night People
Port Tropique
Landscape with Traveler
A Boy's Novel
The Sailor & Lula Novels:
    Wild at Heart
    Perdita Durango
    Sailor's Holiday
    Sultans of Africa
    Consuelo's Kiss
    Bad Day for the Leopard Man

Non-Fiction
Out of the Past: Adventures in Film Noir
Las cuatro reinas (with David Perry)
Bordertown (with David Perry)
The Phantom Father: A Memoir
A Day at the Races: The Education of a Racetracker
Saroyan: A Biography (with Lawrence Lee)
The Neighborhood of Baseball
Jack's Book: An Oral Biography of Jack Kerouac (with Lawrence Lee)

Poetry
Back in America
Replies to Wang Wei
Ghosts No Horse Can Carry
Giotto's Circle

Play
Hotel Room Trilogy

Screenplay
Lost Highway (with David Lynch)

Anthology
The Rooster Trapped in the Reptile Room: A Barry Gifford Reader

Brando
Rides
Alone

A Reconsideration of
the Film *One-Eyed Jacks*

Barry Gifford

THE TERRA NOVA SERIES

North Atlantic Books
Berkeley • California

Published by
North Atlantic Books
P.O. Box 12327   Cover and book design by Paula Morrison
Berkeley, California 94712   Printed in the United States of America

Portions of this book were previously published, in different form, in the magazine *Letras Libres* (Mexico City); and in *The Rooster Trapped in the Reptile Room: A Barry Gifford Reader* (New York).

The author wishes to acknowledge the assistance and editorial expertise provided by Rob White of the British Film Institute during the composition of this book. Excerpts from the screenplay *Black Sun Rising* are used with the kind permission of James Hamilton.

Brando Rides Alone: A Reconsideration of the Film One-Eyed Jacks is sponsored by the Society for the Study of Native Arts and Sciences, a nonprofit educational corporation whose goals are to develop an educational and crosscultural perspective linking various scientific, social, and artistic fields; to nurture a holistic view of arts, sciences, humanities, and healing; and to publish and distribute literature on the relationship of mind, body, and nature.

Library of Congress Cataloging-in-Publication Data

Gifford, Barry, 1946–
Brando rides alone : a reconsideration of the film One-eyed jacks / by
Barry Gifford.
        p. cm. — (The terra nova series)
    Includes bibliographical references.
    ISBN 1-55643-485-5
    1. One-eyed jacks (Motion picture) 2. Brando, Marlon—Criticism and
    interpretation. I. Title. II. Series.
    PN1997.O453 G54 2004
    791.43'72—dc22

                                                2003024576

1 2 3 4 5 6 7 8 9 DATA 09 08 07 06 05 04

For Oscar Bucher

... Men die ...
It is a truth—of Blood—
But we—are dying in Drama—
And Drama—is never dead—

—Emily Dickinson

Contents

PART
ONE

"This ring belonged to my mother."
(or, as Proust said, *"Literature is the finest
kind of lying."*)

1. An Unforgettable Film

One-Eyed Jacks (1961). Directed by Marlon Brando. Starring Marlon Brando, Karl Malden, Pina Pellicer, Timothy Carey, Katy Jurado, Ben Johnson, and Elisha Cook, Jr. Screenplay by Guy Trosper and Calder Willingham.

Brando never looked better than he did in this picture; in fact, he made certain—he was the director, after all—that he was downright beautiful, if fat around the edges, a tendency difficult for him to disguise even then. The opening scene is a beauty: Marlon, as Rio, or The Kid, is sweet-talking a classy *señorita* at her house, cooing in her ear and slipping a ring onto the third finger of her left hand, telling her it's the ring his mother gave him just before she died. The dark-eyed beauty melts as he insinuates his body into hers—The Kid knows he's about to carve another notch on his gun. Then Karl Malden, called Dad Longworth, who's been taking care of some business of his own, shows up and shouts that the law is hot on their trail—this is Sonora, Mexico, in 1880—they've got to hightail it pronto! Rio wrenches the ring his "mother" gave him on her deathbed off the *señorita's* finger, says sorry, honey, and splits with his *compadre* Dad, leaving her, with perspiring thighs and quivering lips, in a literal lurch.

Dad and The Kid are bandits, of course, and they take off for the mountains with the gold booty they've appropriated from a Mexican bank. They ride hard for the *sierras* and finally hunker down on a ridge, doing their best to hold off the troops. One of their horses goes down, they're trapped, and Dad goes for help, taking the gold with him while Rio holds his position. He does the best he can, keeps looking over his shoulder for his trusted *compañero* to come back for him, but the authorities close in. Dad's to hell and gone with the loot, betraying The Kid, and Brando surrenders with the bitter knowledge that his so-called best friend has abandoned him.

The Kid breaks jail eventually and, accompanied by a Mexican cellmate, picks up Dad Longworth's stale trail, tracking him to a town on the central California coast near Big Sur. It's been five long years since Dad left Rio for dead on the mountain and Longworth has built himself a new life—with the aid of the stolen gold—he's now a sheriff, married to a handsome Mexican woman played by Katy Jurado (sturdier-looking a decade since her svelte *la victima* in Buñuel's *El Bruto*), and stepfather to Katy's pretty, barely post-adolescent daughter played by Pina Pellicer (who later committed suicide).

When Rio shows up with not only his Mex escapee pal

but a trio of low company, including Ben Johnson playing the kind of badass he did in *Vera Cruz* and *Shane,* old Dad knows The Kid is itching to burn "Vengeance Is Mine" like a racehorse i.d. on the inside of Longworth's upper lip. Not only is Dad nervous about his own safety but that of his wife and daughter and the town bank. The sheriff pretends he's glad to see Rio, amazed he's still alive, tells The Kid a cock and bull story about how he couldn't get back to the mountain, how the gold got away and all sorts of mealy-mouthed bushwah. Rio just takes it easy, slow to rile, seething beneath the surface at Dad's lies. Dad knows Rio knows he's lying, and warns him to behave; this is a nice little town we got here, a good place to raise a family. Yeah, drawls Rio, I might just want to do that. Longworth snickers, says this ain't your kind of situation, Kid. Best if you moved on.

The Kid doesn't move on. He sniffs out Dad's daughter, gets a start on that, then brawls with Timothy Carey, a snarling Neanderthal thug who attacks Rio in a bar. The Kid shoots him dead (in self-defense), and for this Dad nails Rio, hauls him to a hitching post, and in view of the citizens smashes The Kid's gun hand with the butt of a rifle, pulverizing Rio's trigger finger. Dad orders him out of town and Rio limps away with his confederates to bide his time on a beach ranchito while his hand heals.

4

Ben Johnson and his partner Harv (Sam Gilman) deride The Kid's attempts to shoot again once his gun hand is sound enough to rehabilitate, and they're impatient to bust the bank. They don't care much about Rio's revenge motive—until he got hurt they kept a cool distance from him, having heard about The Kid's gunfighting prowess; but now he's damaged goods and they've got big doubts that Rio will ever be of real use to them. Disrespect doesn't pay off for much in a world of killers, of course, and The Kid does come back. All of the mean business we've been waiting for is played out to no good end, and it's worth the wait. There's a particularly chilling moment when Rio's jailfriend is turned on by the bad brothers, but the scene itself is so poetically and beautifully set on the windswept, cypress-spotted sand dunes of the Monterey coast that the grisly part almost doesn't matter. In fact, the California littoral is a major player in the movie, making even the few tedious parts bearable. It's a long'un: 141 minutes of Brando's fumbling and mumbling, but it works, and often majestically.

According to film editor Paul Seydor, one of the first full-length screenplays Sam Peckinpah ever wrote was an adaptation of *The Authentic Death of Hendry Jones,* a novel by Charles Neider (1956), which was based on the lives of Pat Garrett and Billy the Kid. Neider set his story not in New Mexico, where Pat and Billy had known each other, but in

California, and fictionalized Billy Bonney and Pat Garrett as Hendry Jones and Dad Longworth. Garrett had written a book called *The Authentic Life of Billy the Kid* from which, also according to Seydor (who was a great friend and *confrère* of Peckinpah's), Neider borrowed, lifting dialogue and various incidents. Peckinpah was hired to direct the film version in 1957, wrote the screenplay, which went through numerous vicissitudes, then was fired off the project.

Following Peckinpah's departure—he would go on to direct an unhappy version of these events, *Pat Garrett and Billy the Kid* in 1973—five or six other director/writers, including Stanley Kubrick (who found Brando to be a less-than-candid and/or trustworthy piece of work), came and went, until finally, in 1960, Marlon Brando—who owned the book rights—directed the picture, ultimately re-titled *One-Eyed Jacks.* Brando's opus isn't Billy Bonney's story— Arthur Penn, in 1958, gave it a try with *The Left-Handed Gun,* Paul Newman re-creating his role from TV's *Philco Playhouse* (though James Dean was supposed to have starred in the movie), with a screenplay by Gore Vidal; it was Stan Dragoti, in 1972, who made the best Billy the Kid film by far, *Dirty Little Billy* with Michael J. Pollard as a whiney, mud-splattered, mutt-faced, cowardly, backshooting punk killer—but Brando did a splendid job, bringing together a story of almost-epic proportions, using the big screen to

6

force surrender as real cinema demands. That Brando never again directed a movie may or may not have been a good thing, but with *One-Eyed Jacks* he accomplished what more celebrated directors could seldom do: he made an unforgettable film. After he saw Paramount's final cut, however, Brando said: "Any pretension I've sometimes had of being artistic is now just a long, chilly hope."

One-Eyed Jacks is not a masterpiece, like Peckinpah's *The Wild Bunch,* but I'll always remember Brando's Rio, The Kid, goading Malden's Dad Longworth—these two had had it out before in *A Streetcar Named Desire* (1951)—"How you doin', Dad?" The Kid asks, fake-friendly, when he arrives in Sheriff Longworth's town, suppressing his hatred of the father figure he once loved and trusted who'd thrown him to the wolves. It may as well have been the poet saying, "How do you like your blue-eyed boy now, mister death?"

2. Brando

Where to begin with Marlon Brando? Arguably, Brando was the first authentic American movie star who had also been a great success in the theater. I never saw him on stage but his rep from *Truckline Cafe* and *A Streetcar Named Desire* precedes him to *The Men,* his first movie, in which he portrayed a paraplegic. In retrospect this seemed an off choice to me for Brando to have made for his film debut. It was a solid, down to earth, unsensational role, and my respect for Brando initially stemmed from this performance. The only other person I remember being in the movie is Jack Webb, of *Dragnet* fame—who, by the way, was terrific in *The Last Time I Saw Archie* and Billy Wilder's *Sunset Boulevard,* an underrated actor. After *The Men* Marlon made the film of *Streetcar* and *The Wild One,* which tore it for the old folks and the squares but thrilled the kids, even though Lee Marvin, as Brando's rival motorcycle gang leader, stole the movie. By the time (1954) Brando did *On the Waterfront,* he was an indelible icon in the pantheon of American Culture Vulturehood. "I coulda been a contenduh. I coulda been *some-body*," he complained to Rod Steiger as his brother, Charlie, in the back seat of an automobile *with a Venetian blind over the rear window!* "Instead of a bum, which is what I am." As the brokendown pug, Terry Molloy, who was forced by Charlie and his gangster cohorts to take a dive so that they could go for the price on Wilson, the lucky stiff beneficiary of the fix, Brando edged toward immortality. But then he played in a long string of losing games (though I thought *Bedtime Story,* an overlooked comedy with David Niven, was a tiny riot), not really insuring his status among the gods until *Last Tango in Paris* and *The Godfather.* I've had European actors tell me they think Brando is "too obvious" a performer—to hell with them and their opinions picked out of the ashes of burnt-out cultures. Marlon Brando made Americans, in their wretched void of seemingly purposeful ignorance and dreamy nostalgias for places and times that never existed, *feel* something outside of themselves. Sure, he got grotesquely fat and Truman Capote called him an idiot and his son murdered his daughter's lover and then she killed herself and he had several wives and who knows how many children and he probably became clinically crazy years and years ago, but the guy did a lot of work that people will remember for a long time if not for always, and anyway he's from Libertyville, Illinois (though born in Omaha), where I used to go swimming with my mother when I was a kid, and I remember the farms there, which are now suburban Chicago housing developments. Brando undoubtedly remembers the farms that were there, too, he lived on one, and Orson Welles was from rural Illinois, also. Homeboys, all homeboys, filled with longing, looking to create other worlds, and Brando did it despite what those lousy European actors say dropping cigarette butts into their espresso cups.

3. Timothy Carey

Now here's a character, a real character let alone a character actor. I'll never, ever forget Timothy Carey as the rifleman who shoots and kills the racehorse in Kubrick's *The Killing,* or as the mob thug in Cassavetes' *The Killing of a Chinese Bookie,* and certainly not as the drunken lout in *One-Eyed Jacks.* With a lock of lank black hair always falling over one eye, Carey careened around menacingly in whatever context he appeared. His voice was deep but sounded as if he were always gargling, words bubbling up, burping at his listeners. Carey was big and darkly depraved looking—out of control scary, which often made him seem worse than Lawrence Tierney's troubled personae. If little kids saw him lurching along the sidewalk headed their way, they'd abandon their toys and run. I saw him on a latenight TV talk show, wearing a too-small Hawaiian shirt, detailing for the horrified host his life's work: the study of flatulence. He was deranged, not dangerous, I guessed. Tom Luddy, who worked for Francis Coppola, once gave me, for a reason I no longer remember, Timothy Carey's address and telephone number, which I still have in my directory—he lived in El Monte, California—but I never got in touch with him other than telepathically, and a few years ago he died. In an essay I wrote about an absurd little 1955 movie called *Finger Man,* I described Carey as being unequaled at The Unbridled Snarl. He couldn't control his hands or his hair. He justified the French intellectual's image of the typical American male. And just what do I know about how French intellectuals think? you may well ask. And while you're at it, exactly what—or who—is a typical American male?

4 Katy Jurado, Pina Pellicer, & Other Mexican Actresses

When referred to in magazine and newspaper articles, Katy Jurado was most always called the Fiery Katy Jurado. She played Gary Cooper's mistress in *High Noon* and the wife of Spencer Tracy in *Broken Lance* and, of course, the wife of Karl Malden in *One-Eyed Jacks.* In real life she was married for a time to the actor Ernest Borgnine, who called her "a tiger," but she always was a Mexican citizen. Katy never went Hollywood, she lived in Cuernavaca. She worked for Luis Buñuel in 1952 in his heavyhanded slice of life *El Bruto,* when she had her looks. She never rivalled Dolores Del Rio or Maria Félix or even Rita Moreno, Isela Vega or Movita (one of Marlon's wives) in the Drop Dead department, but Katy Jurado was always a convincing actress, even as Elvis Presley's mother. (In *Stay Away, Joe.*) Dolores Del Rio was in *Flaming Star,* making Elvis probably the only American actor from Tupelo, Mississippi, to play opposite two Mexican movie stars in the 1960s. Jurado brought an air of dignity and intelligence to her film roles. I always believed that her character was smarter than any other character in the movie. And for some reason it pleased me to read in her obituary that she had a daughter who lived in Chicago.

Pina Pellicer died by her own hand very young. She was

a lover of Brando's, who wrote in his autobiography that during the filming of *One-Eyed Jacks* he "slept with a lot of pretty women and had a lot of laughs." Pina Pellicer looked pretty fragile, pretty and fragile, on-screen. I can't imagine life to her was a lot of laughs. I don't know anything about her, really, but in the movie she seems frightened and shy, the opposite of Katy Jurado, who played her mother. The only Mexican movie star I know is Salma Hayek, who seems quite adept at handling herself and getting along with people. I acted in a scene with her in a film in Venice, Italy, and Salma blew through it like a tiny tornado. She knew exactly what to do and how to do it well. My guess is that Pina Pellicer never possessed that kind of confidence, the kind you need to keep going. One of Maria Félix's five husbands was the great Mexican songwriter Agustin Lara, who sat at home at the piano in Mexico City and composed sad, heartbreaking laments ("Noche de Ronda," "Veracruz," "Solamente una vez," "Maria Bonita"—about Maria Félix) while his actress wife flamboyantly philandered around the world. And Orson Welles, having left his wife, Rita Hayworth, for Dolores Del Rio, pronounced Pains of the River the most beautiful woman in the world, but he didn't marry her.

5. Karl Malden

The best nose in the business. Malden's proboscis looked like it had been fought over and chewed on and pitted and pulled and pried and done got elongated by a pride of lions wrestling over the last morsel on the plains of the Serengeti. Malden *intruded* into scenes several seconds after his nose entered the frame. Okay, enough about his schnozz. He was a heavy actor, a large gesture in a roomful of nuances. Stuck close to Brando: *Streetcar, Waterfront, Jacks.* I liked him in *The Cincinnati Kid,* another film almost directed by Sam Peckinpah (who got fired at the start). In *Cincinnati* he's got a sexy young wife, played by Ann-Margret, who cheats on him with Steve McQueen. (Can't imagine why.) Malden was always second fiddle but a block of granite nonetheless. I could imagine him playing on the offensive line at Rutgers with Vince Lombardi. When Stanley Kubrick said to Marlon Brando that he'd read the script for *One-Eyed Jacks* but couldn't understand what the movie was about, Brando told him: "This picture is about my having to pay two hundred and fifty thousand dollars a week to Karl Malden." Brando had signed Malden up, and each week the filming was delayed meant another $250,000 lost. Kubrick responded, "Well, if that's what it's about, I think I'm doing the wrong picture." So Kubrick didn't direct, and Sidney Lumet and Elia Kazan turned it down, too. Peckinpah never got an offer, and was even aced out of the screenplay credit. Apparently Brando dumped Peckinpah for Kubrick (who was only 29), and when Kubrick bailed Brando had indeed to justify the commitment to Karl Malden or head for Teti'aroa (which he did later). Malden did a wonderful job as Dad Longworth—he knew just how to *appraise* Rio, how not only to look but to look *at.* As Rio's surrogate father he knew exactly how to make him squirm, despite his having ditched and left The Kid for good as dead back in the day. Malden knew how to put the mean into meaning and the meaning into mean, something a handsome man couldn't do.

6. Ben Johnson

A real cowboy, Ben Johnson was brought west from Texas by Howard Hughes in the 1940s to take care of his horses. He wound up in the movies and just about became a movie star. Hughes bought RKO so that he could date actresses, which he did by the boatload, and he even married a few. I don't have any idea what Ben Johnson's love life was like, but he maintained his sly-eyed good looks while working for John Ford, George Stevens, Brando, and dozens of others, capping his career with not only an Academy Award-winning performance for Peter Bogdanovich in *The Last Picture Show,* but slightly earlier for the man Marlon jilted, Sam Peckinpah, in *The Getaway* in 1972. In that film based on a Jim Thompson novel, Johnson had the face and demeanor of a cruel wolf, torturer of Steve McQueen and Ali McGraw, forcing them to grovel until they turn on him. By this time Ben Johnson knew just how to act, to keep a tension, to keep a hate on. But Johnson was at his very best in Peckinpah's *The Wild Bunch* (1969), for my money the best American movie ever made. He and Warren Oates play the Gorch brothers, Lyle and Tector—violent, whoring, harddrinking, murderous, mothergrabbing sonsofbitches— but *loyal* mothergrabbing sonsofbitches, loyal to their ethos, their notion by God or the devil of what Right just might could be. When Ben and Warren join William Holden and Ernest Borgnine in their Mexican Death March from the whorehouse to General Mapache's hangout, hellbound and *certain* because this is the end of the only way of life they know is worth living, they have no choice, and I look each time into Ben Johnson's eyes and he's got me fooled because I know he ain't acting in that moment, he's right there square in the narrow corner not called No Turning Back for nothing. Brando used Johnson to good advantage in *Jacks,* keeping him on the back burner while Brando did his star turn. Johnson goaded Brando good, he kept in character—but then Peckinpah and Bogdanovich took the halter off of Hughes's daddy's cowhand. Ben Johnson put his own brand on the movies. You can't miss it.

7. Slim Pickens & Elisha Cook, Jr.

The most famous ride Slim Pickens ever took was on the nuclear bomb at the end of Kubrick's film, *Dr. Strangelove.* Like Ben Johnson, Pickens was a cowhand and rodeo performer brought to Hollywood to lend western movies a degree of authenticity. In *One-Eyed Jacks* he distinguished himself by portraying a craven deputy whom Rio bluffs with an unloaded Derringer into unlocking his cell door. Pickens transforms himself from a leering, wise-cracking, bullying liar into a crawling coward in a flick of an eyelash, his weak receded double chin quivering, Adam's apple palpitating as Brando humiliates him and locks Pickens up in his own jail. A regular in western movies for decades, Slim Pickens became an accomplished comic actor—note his performance in *Rancho Deluxe,* as well as in the aforementioned *Dr. Strangelove.* Terry Southern, Kubrick's screenwriter on *Strangelove,* told this bizarre story about Pickens: When Slim met the African-American actor James Earl Jones on the set, Southern mentioned to Jones that Pickens had just finished filming *One-Eyed Jacks* with Brando. Jones politely inquired as to how it was working with the great Mr. Brando, and countryboy Slim told him, "Wal, you know ah worked with Bud Brando for right near a full year, an' durin' that time ah never seen him do one thing that wudn't *all man* an' *all white*." Pickens had beady eyes, was always in need of a shave, didn't disguise his pot belly, and always made the movie he was in better. Toward the very end of *The Getaway,* he has a brief, wonderful scene with Steve McQueen when he sells his pickup truck to bank robber Doc McCoy and his wife, Carol (Ali McGraw), both of whom he's stopped for on the road. Pickens's character drives a hard bargain but gladly takes an excessive offer from Carol and just gets out on the highway, yells Yahoo!, and ambles bowleggedly away with his bonanza, a grin on his scraggly face the size of Texas, his birthplace.

Elisha Cook, Jr. and Wallace Ford supposedly appeared in more films than any other actors in the history of the movies. Cook made a mark in *The Maltese Falcon, Shane, Born to Kill,* and dozens more. But it's really in Kubrick's masterpiece *The Killing* that Cook cooks the hottest. A parimutuel clerk at the racktrack his gang plans to rob, Cook is married to bombshell Marie Windsor, a devil dame who taunts her husband for not being a good enough provider along with his more obvious shortcomings such as being short, ugly, wimpy, etc. Why did she marry him in the first place? She's a cheap whore who's got a man or more on the side. Cook brags to her about the big heist he and his cohorts are about to pull off, desperate to impress and keep her. She then blabs to a boyfriend about the scam, which causes the thing to blow up. Cook stumbles back to their seedy apartment after the disastrous denouement and murders her. This is his best performance, though Cook was always good, always tortured and pathetic, as weaselly gunsel Wilmer in *Falcon* or a hophead hotel bellboy being chewed to death by anxiety over what he'll never have or be. Elisha Cook, Jr. conveyed what it means to be a Terrified Little Man better than anyone. He lived to be almost a hundred years old.

8. Sam Peckinpah & Stanley Kubrick

Sam Peckinpah had been fascinated by the story of Billy the Kid and Pat Garrett for years and wanted to do a movie about them. In 1956, he decided to write a screenplay based on Charles Neider's novel, *The Authentic Death of Hendry Jones,* which he did, finishing it on November 11, 1957. Brando's Pennebaker Productions bought the book rights and Peckinpah was thrilled at the idea of scripting the picture. On May 12, 1958, Brando's company signed a contract with Stanley Kubrick for him to direct the movie for Paramount Pictures. Peckinpah revised his screenplay and handed it in on May 6, 1959. Kubrick didn't like it, and Brando dumped Peckinpah, who was understandably depressed by this decision. Kubrick hired Calder Willingham to rewrite the screenplay with him but they apparently stalled on page fifty-two and hit a dead end. The film was by now re-titled *One-Eyed Jacks.* Willingham, who (with Jim Thompson) had written *Paths of Glory* for Kubrick, was let go, as was Kubrick, who went to work on *Lolita.* He later said he found Brando to be more than a little disingenuous in his dealings, and Peckinpah had nothing good to say about the finished product. The screenplay credit went to Guy Trosper, who Brando had hired on, and Willingham, though Brando declared that he rewrote virtually all of the script himself with Trosper. Various biographers of Peckinpah and Brando have written that the screenplay bore little or no resemblance to the one crafted by Peckinpah, but I've read his screenplay and it compares favorably to the final version except for the crucial point of making out Malden's character, Dad Longworth, to be a liar along with everybody else. Brando said he lost interest in the film in the editing stage and just let Paramount cut the picture to their satisfaction. Who's lying here? It is incomprehensible to me that Peckinpah was not accorded a credit for the screenplay. By 1973, when he directed *Pat Garrett and Billy the Kid,* his own lethargy doomed the project. (As Jim Hamilton, who worked on the script of *Cross of Iron* (1977) said, *Cross of Iron* was "one of the most fatigue-ridden movies ever made.") It's too bad that Peckinpah couldn't trump Brando with his own treatment of the same subject, but the truth is that *One-Eyed Jacks* is a better film than *Pat Garrett and Billy the Kid,* a lot better. Kubrick never did make a western.

9. Don't Forget to Thank the Producer

Frank Rosenberg, the producer of *One-Eyed Jacks,* died on my birthday, October 18th, in 2002. A well-known actor once asked me, only semi-rhetorically, "What does a producer do?" Most people not intimate with the movie business think that the producer raises the money to get the picture made, and in most cases this is true. But producers do many things having nothing (or everything) to do with money. They cast, write (and re-write), fetch, pamper, persuade, murder, organize, disturb, finagle, fade away, bully, mollycoddle (I've always wanted to use that word), and, if they're really smart, stay out of the way once the ball has begun to roll. Producers such as David O. Selznick (*Gone with the Wind, Duel in the Sun,* etc.) stood in the middle of the road doing everything imaginable. Others just let the director, actors, cameraman, and so on do the job they were hired to do.

It was Frank Rosenberg who hired Sam Peckinpah to write the first draft of *One-Eyed Jacks.* This is significant because it was the very first time Peckinpah had tried his hand at scripting a feature-length film. Rosenberg also gave Jayne Mansfield her start in motion pictures (he obviously understood the meaning of the word "motion"), in *Illegal* in 1955, with Edward G. Robinson and Nina Foch. Here was a producer with an eye for talent—Peckinpah, of course—but Mansfield had talent, too. She was a terrific comedian—dig *Will Success Spoil Rock Hunter?* for example. Under the tutelage of a director like Frank Tashlin, she thrived.

Born in Brooklyn soon after the turn of the 20th century, Frank Rosenberg went to work at sixteen in the shipping department of Columbia Pictures in New York. Columbia's czar, Harry Cohn, tabbed him to run his national publicity and advertising department. In his early forties, Rosenberg moved to Hollywood to helm the Columbia publicity office there, and a few years later he struck out on his own, producing films for Warner Brothers, Twentieth Century-Fox, Columbia, and others. I'll always be indebted to him for producing *King of the Khyber Rifles,* starring Tyrone Power, one of my favorite childhood films. I saw *King of the Khyber Rifles* at the Ciné theater in Chicago in 1953 with my father, who called the star Tyrone Cupcake. My dad did not think highly of most movie stars as human beings. Watching Ty Cupcake as a half-caste British officer commanding Indian cavalry riding against Afghan hordes did not inspire my father to change his opinion. In his business he'd dealt with a lot of Hollywood types, he knew their habits and tendencies and how phony those people were, but he didn't spoil my fantasy; not yet, anyway.

Back to Frank Rosenberg. According to Rosenberg, it

was he who bought the rights to Charles Neider's novel *The Authentic Death of Hendry Jones,* perhaps at Brando's request. In any case, his first writing hire was Rod Serling, creator of the fabulously successful television series *The Twilight Zone.* Serling did an adaptation of the novel, which Rosenberg rejected, and he then turned to Peckinpah. Bloody Sam did a better job and Brando went for it right away, but as we know once Marlon's pudgy fingers got into the goo Peckinpah was soon removed from the mix.

The important part of all this is to remember that Rosenberg got the movie made. He did what he had to do even if it meant spooning *menudo* down Marlon Cupcake's throat or getting the seamstress to let out his pants a little (or a lot). Frank Rosenberg also produced the detective drama *Madigan* in 1968 with Richard Widmark, a considerably thinner actor.

PART TWO

Brando Rides Alone

(or *"I'm going to teach you a lesson you'll never forget."*)

Brando Rides Alone

(or *"I'm going to teach you a lesson you'll never forget."*)

In his essay, "The Lesson of the Master," Graham Greene wrote, "No writer has been the victim of more misleading criticism than Henry James.... [He] needed to express his sense of the cruelties and deceptions beneath civilized relationships ... [but] James's problem was to admit violence without becoming violent. He mustn't let violence lend the tone (that is melodrama): violence must draw its tone from all the rest of life; it must be subdued, and it must not, above all, be sudden and inexplicable."

What does Henry James have to do with this discursive *faux*-exegesis of *One-Eyed Jacks?* How does "the master," as Greene called him, a literary Thoroughbred, get herded into the same corral as an ornery Cal-bred cayuse like Timothy Carey? Well, pardner, as far as I'm concerned, HJ ain't got smack over Sam Peckinpah in the Art department. The critic R.P. Blackmur observed that James's argument was "in art what is merely stated is not presented, what is not presented is not vivid, what is not vivid is not represented, and what is not represented is not art." About Blackmur's analysis, Graham Greene succinctly commented, "That is a dogma which no one will dispute."

My aim is to once and for all dismiss from the rhetoric

any distinction between Low Art and High Art. Art is where you find it. In *One-Eyed Jacks* the violence is seldom sudden; neither is it inexplicable. Even The Master may have gotten a charge out of it. *The Wild Bunch* contains as much meaning as *The Portrait of A Lady* or *Wings of the Dove.* When Blackmur used the word "represent" he had no idea that one day it would be a verb. But what I'm really after here is to take on the problem not of whether James in *Washington Square* or *The Aspern Papers* made better use of violence than Brando did in *One-Eyed Jacks,* or whether The Master or The Mumbler succumbed to melodrama. No, it's time to separate reviewers from critics (as Greene was in his essay) and critics from creators by examining from a distance of more than forty years the so-called critical reaction to the film upon its release.

It is important to note that most journalists writing about films have very little time to think about them, let alone see them more than once. (Book reviewers should have no such problem.) That the vast majority of them have no clue as to the purpose of criticism does not really matter since they are under pressure to fill so many column inches in (usually) the following day's newspaper or issue of a magazine about to go to press. Reviewers, therefore, are paid not to think but to write (fast) and opine, no matter how foolish or uninformed their conclusions. Movie reviewers on television are under similar and other pressures—mostly they seem not to want to offend the studios that offer big budget pictures so that they will not be ostracized from future promotional junkets. The threat of being banned from the studio food troughs is beyond their wildest fears. The horror! The horror!

Alexander Walker (an "author" of numerous celebrity biographies) was moved to write in the *Evening Standard* of 15 June 1961, about Brando "squatting in a Method trance by the sea looking for all the world like Narcissus in ranch pants." (Ranch pants?) This sort of condescending archery is not criticism, it's just a snide potshot at an immobile target fired from point blank range. It was meretricious of the *Evening Standard* to allow Walker to call himself a film critic; he was merely a silly, mean-spirited person masquerading as a serious journalist. This is the problem even—or even worse—today. At least Walker could sporadically concoct a sprightly sentence.

When Dad Longworth tells Rio, "I'm going to teach you a lesson you'll never forget," just before busting Brando's gun hand with a rifle butt while The Kid's down on his knees tied to a hitching post, it's a sentiment not unlike what I imagine many of these so-called critics vow to themselves (a few even mumbling á la Marlon) before having at the immediate object of their envy or spite. A performer is always at risk, being at the mercy of those creatures out to protect the public from bad books, movies, music, et al. The public doesn't need this kind of protection; they can take care of themselves. Having said all of this, I do want to go on record as acknowledging that exceptions to the rule do exist. There are a few—a very few—good reviewers/critics out there, and they know who they are (or think they do!).

It's interesting to peruse the British reviews of *One-Eyed Jacks* just to see how the subject of violence, physical violence, is treated. Derek Hill, writing in the *Tribune,* was appalled by what he termed "the film's *appetite* for violence." (My italics.) "Extraordinarily efficient, *One-Eyed Jacks* still seems to me a vicious film. Its splendid performances, including Brando's hypnotic hero and the subtly forceful heroine of Pina Pellicer, its breathtaking locations, and its bold borrowings from the best of the silent cinema can't compensate for the sheer nastiness of its outlook." (Is it really nastier in its outlook than The Master's *What Maisie Knew,* published in 1897? Perhaps Hill didn't read it.)

Derek Hill's remarks are revealing of the period, coming six and eight years, respectively, before *Bonnie and Clyde* and *The Wild Bunch,* bloody but poetic takes on nastiness that must have driven Hill into a monastery. One thing neither the creepy Walker nor the ambivalent Hill talk about is the dialogue, much of which I admire, regardless of who really wrote it. After Rio kills the thug portrayed by Carey,

Dad confronts the Kid, who explains to the sheriff, "We took to scufflin' and he come out from behind there with that scatter gun. He didn't give me no selection." It's after this that Longworth serves up his lesson.

Later, while Rio is recuperating at Punta del Diablo, endeavoring to regain his shooting touch, Dad's daughter, Louisa, visits The Kid to tell him he has made her pregnant. When Bob Amory (Ben Johnson) refers to Louisa as "a little jumpin' bean" who might have worn (Johnson says "wore") Rio out so as to render him useless for the bank robbery, Brando busts him one and barks, "Get up, you scum-suckin' pig. . . . You mention her once more and I'm gonna tear your arms out!" This is terrific, if semi-comic stuff; you can see Brando burn when he snarls this admonition. The good part is that Johnson doesn't cower—he's just biding his time until they take the bank in Monterey, then he'll have it out with pretty boy.

Good dialogue is always hard to come by. Most directors get away with clumsy talk by using the camera to distract the viewer. I always remember Ezra Pound, in his *Cantos,* quoting Aubrey Beardsley and William Butler Yeats. When Yeats asked Beardsley why he painted such horrors, Beardsley replied, "Beauty is difficult, Yeats." In *One-Eyed Jacks* there is a surprising surfeit of what sounds true. Another good example comes on the beach the morning after Rio has seduced Louisa and taken her virginity as part of his vendetta against her stepfather. "I don't have no work," he confesses. "I make my livin' robbin' banks.... Everything I told you about last night was lies.... It ain't gonna help much to say it, but I shamed you. And I wish to God I hadn't." Hearing this, Pina Pellicer, resembling the wounded bird she evidently was, looks directly into Brando's eyeslits and delivers this dagger: "You only shame yourself." This works, accompanied as it is by the contrapuntal slap of the "damn waves" Bob Amory complains about "floppin' in and out" all day.

Isabel Quigly, a serious schoolmarm of High Purpose scribbling about "cinema" in *The Spectator* of 23 June 1961, used her two-column page to chastise Brando for having the nerve to risk extending himself from actor (she calls him "less an actor than a presence") to director. (She evidently had more time to cogitate over this than that snippety Walker person.) "Will people in thirty years find [Brando] ludicrous—slouch, mumble, pregnant silences, dazzling though heavy looks [?], lowering gait [?], oppressiveness and all?" (Most of those question marks are mine.) "But now he directs," Quigly correctly states, creating "every situation in *Teach Yourself Westerns* ... enormously self-conscious ... embarrassingly inept ... [and] Brando's stoutness, quite apart from his obvious age, is really too much for one to

accept him as a limber sapling. . . ." (Strange, I never thought
of Brando as a sapling, either.) In closing, the charming Ms.
Quigly (though she was not then, in 1961, a Ms.) informs
her readers that "The film's real limitation is its banality . . .
the characters behave like dummies, not people. . . ." She
likes the natural scenery (Kodak moments. Probably she
went bonkers over Walter Keane's bug-eyed kid paintings.)
and identifies Pina Pellicer as "an original new heroine . . .
brown and birdlike . . . certainly a frontal assault, if nothing else is [Does she mean in the movie or in the greater
world?], on the temple of glamour." Bust my britches if the
left-handed Dame Quigly didn't get rude and racist right
quickly, even if she did go for the idea. (We'll never know.)
Talk about "frontal assault." Back in the day, the sun never
set on the British Empire, Britannia ruled the waves and
philistines such as Isabel-baby were given their column
inches in which to pontificate and cackle like Gagool. All
I've got to say to the memory of old lady Quigly today is,
"Don't look now, honey, but them brown folks is not only
runnin' 'cross y'all's lawn but trippin' down the runways in
Paris and Milan. And guess what else, sweetie? The sun
done set its big bright ass all *over* the British Empire.

Irreverence has its place, especially in, as Isabel Quigly
might have called it, the temple of cinema. So does de-
construction, which is not my game or aim. Let's leave our

Narcissus alone now, where he is happiest, unchallenged in his appraisal. Brando did the best he could and it ain't bad. If you don't believe me, and even if you do, take a look-see for yourself.

A last blast at the critics: The director *(Like Water for Choco-late)* and actor *(The Wild Bunch)* Alfonso Arau told me the following story over dinner one night in San Sebastian, Spain. Mexico's most famous (along with Luis Buñuel)—certainly most infamous—director, Emilio Fernandez, known as "El Indio" because of his mother's origins, made many unforgettable films, several featuring María Félix *(Enamorada)* or Dolores Del Rio (*María Candelária,* called by Beatriz Reyes Nevares "the classic and most memorable of all Mexican films"); he also directed a version of John Steinbeck's story *The Pearl/La Perla,* starring Pedro Armendáriz. Fernandez was born in 1904 in a mining town, Del Hondo, in the state of Coahuila, a wild region torn by revolution, his father's place; El Indio's mother, Sara Romo, was from El Nacimiento, an area occupied by Black Indians, the fugitive Seminoles comprised of black slaves and Southern Creeks who made their way from Florida to Texas then escaped across the border and founded a town called Nacimiento de los Negros, which still exists today.

El Indio's heavy-eyebrowed, leathery, pouchy, powerful face is etched indelibly into the American consciousness because of his appearances in Peckinpah's movies *The Wild Bunch,* in which he portrays the *borracho* nightmare of a revolutionary Mexican general named Mapache, and *Bring Me the Head of Alfredo García,* as the vindictive father of a disgraced daughter who gives the titular order.

Arau told me that after completing a new film Fernandez invited to dinner at his *estancia* the most prominent film critics from Mexico City. After dinner and undoubtedly many drinks, El Indio screened for them his latest effort, then solicited their opinions. One after another, the critics, stuffed and glowing from whiskey and Tequila, praised the film, telling their host what he wanted to hear, that it was his best to date, possibly another masterpiece, as moving as *María Candelaria.* Then a journalist rose and begged to differ, not impolitely, but making clear his opinion that the new movie, while reasonably effective as melodrama, was not a particularly worthy addition to the maestro's *oeuvre.* A silence fell over the room. El Indio, initially uncomprehending and a good two-and-a-half sheets to the wind, finally realized that he was being disrespected on his own turf and drew from beneath his coat a revolver. Without hesitating, he shot the disputatious fool, killing him in front of his fellow guests.

Arau said that for the offense of murdering a critic Fernandez was forced to spend some time in jail (where he was well treated), but since he was a national hero, and the insulting behavior of the deceased was compounded by the fact that at the time of the incident he had been availing himself of El Indio's hospitality, the director's sentence was cut short. Emilio Fernandez is a legend. (He died in 1986.) Nobody remembers the name of the dead critic.

EPILOGUE

Prelude: The Decline of the West/ern
   (or *Apologies to Oswald Spengler*)
+ An excerpt from *Black Sun Rising*
   A screenplay by Barry Gifford & James Hamilton

Prelude to the Epilogue
The Decline of the West/ern

(or *Apologies to Oswald Spengler*)

Popular opinion seems to be that the western as a genre has had its day, that the sun has set on Sunset Carson, Lash LaRue, Hoot Gibson, Johnny Mack Brown, and Red Ryder. John Ford, Howard Hawks, and, finally, Sam Peckinpah, certainly had their way for a spell, didn't they? What really happened is that Americans ran out of West to run to. Even movies became post-modern—no range was free anymore, nor was it home. Oh, every once in a blue moon a good piece of work like *Unforgiven* will turn up; but *The Wild Bunch* signalled the end of the line. The West is now about drive-by shootings in L.A., not drawdowns in Miss Kitty's saloon or over to the O.K. corral. Of Cormac McCarthy's exegeses about the Southwest, the one novel that should be filmed is his gory masterpiece, *Blood Meridian;* instead, a runny-nosed version of McCarthy's *All the Pretty Horses,* a vastly lesser work, was made. The Hollywood studios don't seem willing any longer to take a chance on a "real" western, fearing that no young people will go to see it. Maybe they're right.

Ornery coyote that I am, I roped Jim Hamilton, a survivor of Peckinpah's gang, into collaborating with me on a screenplay based on the history of the Black Seminoles, a unique piece of Americana (and Mexicana) that takes place in 1851. If Ford, Hawks, or Peckinpah were alive and in favor at the studios these days, I'd do my best to persuade them to give our handiwork a shot. *Black Sun Rising,* as Jim Hamilton and I call it, has elements found in *Red River, Wagon Master, Vera Cruz, The Wild Bunch, Bring Me the Head of Alfredo Garcia,* and yes, *One-Eyed Jacks,* as well as many other so-categorized westerns that we admire; but with a little twist and—as Preston Sturges admonished in his *Sullivan's Travels*—a little sex in it. I offer an excerpt of it here, in provisional form, as a tribute to those who have ridden this trail before us.

BLACK SUN RISING

Original Screenplay
by
Barry Gifford & James Hamilton

November 15, 2001
First Draft
[Excerpt]

BLACK SUN RISING

FADE IN:

A BLACK SLAVE WOMAN and her TWO CHILDREN are bathing in a shallow stream near a stand of cottonwood trees. It is a hot, dusty afternoon. The children laugh and play in the shallow water. The mother watches them affectionately, but at the same time she keeps a wary eye on her surroundings. Like the children, she, too, is naked. One of the kids is a boy around ten, the other a girl perhaps seven.

Now the words "MEXICO, 1851, NEAR THE TEXAS BORDER" appear on the screen, followed immediately by:

Thunderous SOUND of horses galloping, coming closer.

Two WHITE MEN on horseback explode out of nowhere, shattering the idyllic scene, and bear down on the mother and her children. One of the riders swoops up the boy onto his saddle, the other does the same with the girl, and they ride furiously across the stream. The mother tries to throw herself in front of one of the horses. She is knocked down, flounders in the water but makes no sound. The kidnappers disappear over the edge of the arroyo and are gone.

CUT TO:

1   EXT.—A STRETCH OF DESERT—DAY

The mother, in a burlap shift but still barefoot, runs across the desert in long powerful strides, sweat pouring from her body. She has recovered from her panic, her face is calm, even resolute.

CUT TO:

2   EXT.—A SEMINOLE INDIAN ENCAMPMENT—ESTABLISHING— DAY

An interracial tribe of CREEK INDIANS and RUNAWAY SLAVES known as MASCOGOS, numbering approximately four hundred, have established a camp at the mouth of a rugged, mesquite-filled canyon called El Moral. These are remnants of the people who have survived the long Seminole Wars in Florida and are now living as fugitives in Mexico.

As they go about their business two men who are leaders of the two factions watch over them.

One is an imposing man of striking dignity named JOHN JULY, one-quarter Creek Indian the rest American Negro; the other man astride a horse a short distance away goes by the name CAPTAIN COYOTE, a full-blooded Creek warrior. He is a moody, unpredictable man about John's age, mischievous and playful one minute, somber and deadly the next. Both men are natural born leaders.

ANGLE ON THE MOTHER

—racing into the encampment, staggering from exhaustion. Members of the tribe rush to her side. John and Coyote immediately assume command; apparently this is not a new development. The war party, three Indians, three Blacks, leap on their horses and ride off. The rest of the Seminoles immediately begin caring for the woman while John July looks on with saddened eyes.

3   EXT.—NEAR THE BORDER—DAY

The Seminoles are doing what they do best—using their tracking skills. One of them points toward the side of the arroyo, makes another sign, and the party splits in two.

4   EXT.—THE RIO GRANDE RIVER—DAY

The two white slavers are loping their horses easily along the banks of the river. The children have submitted.

Suddenly, three of the Seminoles appear at a gallop. The two hunters spur their horses into the river and start across in the shallow water toward the Texas border, riding hard. Now the other three Seminoles are seen approaching from another angle, having circled around to take the men by surprise.

The two slavers ride in circles for a moment, realizing they have no chance. They throw the children into the river and ride hard for the opposite bank on the Texas side.

ANOTHER ANGLE

The Seminoles fire their rifles at the slavers but don't hit them, then they gather up the children and head for home.

5   EXT.—THE RIVER—DAY

The two slavers halt their horses across the river and watch the Seminoles ride away. After a few moments, the slavers resignedly turn their mounts and head north into Texas.

BEGIN CREDITS

CUT TO:

6   EXT.—THE DUPUY RANCH, BRACKETTVILLE, TEXAS—DAY

—as the CREDITS CONTINUE ROLLING. Everything about this spread suggests neatness and cleanliness to an almost severe degree—immaculate ranch-house surrounded by a manicured lawn and garden, with a white-picket fence, outbuildings, barns, etc. Even the cattle grazing nearby look like they're part of an ordered world.

7   INT.—THE STABLES—DAY

SONNY OSCEOLA is grooming a horse. He is in his mid-twenties, a Seminole Indian of mixed white and Creek blood and an exile from both worlds. He is a cool-looking customer, wary, alert, with a certain regal air.

8   EXT.—THE RANCH—DAY

TERESA DUPUY rides in and halts her horse. She shades her eyes from the sun and looks toward the barn, then at the house as if she thinks she might be seen.

TERESA

Sonny! Sonny, where in blazes are you?!

ANOTHER ANGLE

Teresa dismounts and ties her horse up. She looks toward the stables and a slow grin breaks across her face. Teresa is twenty-five or so but could pass for older. She is hatless and tosses her long unruly hair back and heads for the stables, and it is this walk that defines her character in many ways: the long, easy strides of a physical, sexually precocious young woman, horsey and headstrong.

9   INT.—THE STABLES—DAY

Sonny stands just inside the entrance, secretly watching the same thing we've been watching. He grins and turns away, goes back to grooming the horse. We HEAR Teresa's boots crunching on the ground, closer and closer; Sonny pretends he doesn't know she's coming—until—

—Teresa slips under THE HORSE'S NECK and kisses him full on the mouth—a hard, open-mouthed, possessive kiss.

TERESA

You saw me, didn't you? Why didn't you answer?

She nuzzles him, bites his ear, presses closer.

SONNY

I got better things to do than watch you.

TERESA

Liar!

They kiss hotly, then Sonny breaks away.

SONNY

Hey, your old man's about due.

10 INT.—THE TACK ROOM—DAY

A small room cluttered with horse paraphernalia and the reek of old leather. This is where Sonny lives as a hired hand. He and Teresa burst into the room, clutching and kissing, tearing at each other's clothes with erotic abandon, struggling to get their boots off. They start on a cot but end up writhing around on the floor, Teresa on top one moment, Sonny the next. There is an urgency to their love-making, a desperation, without tenderness.

DISSOLVE TO:

11 INT.—THE TACK ROOM—LATER

Sonny and Teresa lie in each other's arms, spent, exhausted, their sexual passion now replaced with great intimacy.

ON SONNY

—as a kind of shadow darkens his face. Teresa doesn't see this change but she feels it. She stiffens, without even looking at him:

> **TERESA**
>
> Where'd you go?

> **SONNY**
>
> Huh—?

> **TERESA**
>
> You were just here and then you weren't. What's wrong?

SONNY

Nothin's wrong.

TERESA

Sonny . . .

SONNY

We can't keep doing this. I'll end up with a load
of buckshot in my ass. Or worse.

TERESA

You're lying. You're not afraid of him.

*He studies her for a moment; she's right—he isn't afraid of her
father, but she's another matter.*

TERESA (cont'd)

Come on—you don't have to hold back with me.
You know that.

SONNY

The tribes are in Mexico, not far from the border.

TERESA

Are you sure?

SONNY

Yeah. I ran into two Seminoles the other day in
Eagle Pass. More'n three hundred of 'em are

down there now. They refused to stay on the reservation in Oklahoma.

He looks closely at her.

TERESA

Jesus . . . all the way from Florida.

He nods.

Teresa gets up and starts dressing quickly.

TERESA (cont'd)

Come on. Let's go talk by the creek.

12 EXT.—ANOTHER PART OF THE RANCH—DAY

Sonny and Teresa have saddled up their horses and are riding out just as her father, CASS DUPUY, and his close friend, ROYCE BOX, come loping in on their horses. Dupuy motions for them to stop. Dupuy is around fifty, a hard-looking man as befits a retired captain in the Texas Rangers.

Royce Box, his sidekick and understudy, is fifteen years younger, also a former Ranger, a very physical, quiet man with a hooded, reined-in look. Taken together, these two men have no doubt struck fear into the hearts of the wayward and the lawless.

DUPUY

What's this?

TERESA

Just moseyin' out for a little ride.

Dupuy crosses one leg over his saddle, takes out his snuff box, and starts packing his lower gum, all the while eyeing both of them, back and forth. That bulging lower lip gives him a peculiar menace.

DUPUY

(to Sonny)

Ain't you got chores?

SONNY

Just shoed this little mare. Thought I'd loosen her up.

Throughout this tense exchange Royce Box has been staring at Teresa in a certain proprietary way that even he's not aware of.

TERESA—ROYCE'S POV

But what has caught Royce's attention is Teresa's dishevelled state and also a loose piece of straw clinging to her hair after her recent carnal interlude. He shoots an apprehensive glance at Dupuy to see if he's noticed but Dupuy is busy eyeballing

Sonny. Royce now shifts his attention to Sonny as well, open hostility in his eyes.

DUPUY

See you're back quick.

He leans out over his saddle, spits a gob of snuff juice, as Sonny and Teresa pass.

13 EXT.—A CREEK-BED—DAY

The creek is no more than about four feet wide this time of year but it's a secluded, pretty site, with a few cottonwood trees, where their horses are tethered in the shade. Sonny is tossing pebbles into the water; Teresa sits down on the grassy bank and stares at the gently flowing stream.

TERESA

So that's why my Daddy and Royce and them been crossin' the border at night.

SONNY

They're slave-hunters.

TERESA

Well, never mind Daddy. What I'm asking you is, would you trust the Mexican government? They got a revolution every other day down there. How can they keep promises? Besides which, they

54

won't give your people land out of the goodness
of their hearts.

SONNY

True.

TERESA

How long have they been in Mexico?

SONNY

I don't know. Not long. They left Florida damn
near two years ago. Many died on the trail—
starvation, fighting other tribes, sickness. There's
a mess of Mascogos travellin' with 'em, too.

TERESA

Mascogos?

SONNY

They're black slaves who ran away from
plantations in Georgia and Alabama, then
crossed into Florida when the Spanish owned it
and lived among the Seminoles, who were mostly
breakaway Creeks. Some even intermarried. They
fought the government right alongside the
Seminoles. A lot of 'em spoke good English and
knew how to read between the lines of a treaty.
Seminole means to break off, to secede . . .

TERESA

I never heard of slaves and Indians livin' together before.

SONNY

Some whites, too. My grandfather, William Powell, was a white trader.

TERESA

These two men you saw—did you tell them who you are?

Sonny sits down next to her.

SONNY

Naw. They just figured I was some border breed.

Teresa moves as close to him as she can get. She runs her hand lightly through his hair.

TERESA

But you're the son of Osceola, a Seminole Chief.

SONNY

They wouldn't have believed me—

TERESA

—leader of an undefeated people.
    (a beat)

But you weren't one of them, one of the
undefeated. That's what's been eating away at
you all these years, hasn't it?

Sonny shrugs. She lays her head in the crook of his shoulder.

TERESA (cont'd)
You should be proud. I wish I had Indian blood
in me.

SONNY
I like your blood just fine.

TERESA
(almost under her breath)
—Instead of what I got.

SONNY
Teresa—you have to stop talkin' that way. You
got your mother's blood in you, too, don't forget.

Teresa feels a mood shift coming on, and looks away.

SONNY (cont'd)
You never did tell me how she died.

TERESA
(a long beat)
Her heart froze over. Listen, Sonny, would you

mind riding on back to the ranch without me? I
need to be alone for a while.

14 EXT.—A SMALL LAKE ON THE DUPUY RANCH—DAY

*Teresa is riding her horse slowly along the grassy edge of the
water. The horse is limping noticeably and she dismounts, checks
the horse's ailing hoof, sees that he's thrown a shoe. She looks
OFF—*

ANOTHER ANGLE

*—at a tiny knoll of dry land in the middle of the lake, with a
willow tree growing out of it. She is enchanted by the solitude
of the setting. She starts walking her horse toward home, her
head down, absorbed by her thoughts.*

ON ROYCE BOX

*He happens to be riding past the lake but has not seen Teresa.
Now he glances sharply at the ground near the grassy bank,
sees some tracks, and follows them until—*

TERESA

*comes into view. He rides up alongside her. She looks up and
smiles at him.*

> ROYCE

He throw you?

TERESA

Naw. Just a worn-out shoe. Put a little split in his hoof.

ROYCE

(indicates his saddle)
Want to climb on? I'll see you home.

TERESA

I'd just as soon walk, thank you.

ROYCE

I never was much for walkin'. Got on a horse before I could.

TERESA

It's when I do my best thinking.

ROYCE

That a fact? Well, I might give it a go, I guess. If you don't mind.

He dismounts and they walk in silence for a while, leading their horses. Royce has never been alone with her in these circumstances and it shows; but Teresa is comfortable around him, as an extended family member.

ROYCE (cont'd)
Mind if I ask what you're thinkin' about?

Teresa glances at him, surprised by the question. She mulls over an answer.

TERESA

You'd never guess.

ROYCE

You'll have to tell me, then.

TERESA

(a sweeping gesture with her arm)
I was just thinking. . . . What if all this country
was water instead of grassland? What if we were
completely surrounded by water?

ROYCE

You're right—I wouldn't have guessed that's
what was on your mind. You mean, if this was all
one big ol' pond, like that one back there?

TERESA

Yeah. But I think of it as a lake, not a pond. I've
had dreams about that little lake, and they always
make me wish I was somewhere else.

ROYCE

Near an ocean, maybe.

TERESA

I dream about oceans, too. Fact is, for a rancher's daughter I love water a whole lot better than I do country.

ROYCE

Dreamin' about what you can't have.

He glances sidelong at her. She's chewing on a long blade of grass, a million miles away, so he lets his eyes linger on her face.

ROYCE (cont'd)

Well, then. . . . Aw, never mind.

TERESA

What? Go on—don't be shy.

ROYCE

Well, if this was all water and we're here, walkin' along like this, why, then we'd be . . .

(a beat)

. . . on an island.

Teresa looks up at him, delighted with his response.

TERESA

(laughing)

That's right! Just me'n Royce Box, stranded on an island. Who ever would have thought of that?

Royce stifles a grin, turns his head away from her then slaps the reins to his horse hard against his thigh.

CUT TO:

15 EXT.—A HORSE AUCTION—DAY

A fairgrounds scene not unlike a modern-day Farmers' Market on a Saturday afternoon. Crowds of people coming and going, horse and buggies arriving, men on horseback, kids running around, food stalls and other wares are being sold. We hear the voice of the AUCTIONEER above the crowd noises cutting in and out.

AN ARENA

Behind the fairgrounds, where the stock the cowboys and ranchers have brought to town for sale are standing about, tended by various cowboys, Sonny Osceola among them.

ON SONNY

Who is busy preparing a horse for the auctioneer's eye. He has an assistant, a YOUNG MEXICAN, helping him. There is a bowl filled with eggs at their feet. His helper breaks them up, stirs them vigorously with a stick.

ROYCE BOX (O.S.)
(in a booming voice filled with sarcasm)

Hey, O-See-Oh-LA! What're you fixin' to do—
serve that horse for breakfast?!

*There's a burst of derisive laughter from Royce's audience. For
just an instant Sonny freezes at hearing his name so grossly
mispronounced; he turns slowly around and looks for Royce.*

ON THE FENCE RAILINGS

*—where Royce is perched, along with several COWBOY
FRIENDS all in a row, watching the action. Royce grins: it's
his show—and the other cowboys are entirely under his influ-
ence. Sonny's eyes move along the row of men, a sort of half-
smile on his face: he's been here before, the smile says.*

SONNY

(to his helper, very low)
Now the egg. Rub hard.

*The helper plunges a sponge into the mixture and begins rubbing
the colt down with it. The horse's coat gleams in the sun and
Sonny looks pleased.*

ROYCE

It appears to be, boys, O-see-oh-LA is tryin' to
cover up somethin', the way he's polishin' that ol'
horse.

ON TWO INDIANS

Who are partly obscured between the railings of the corral, wedged in with some other ONLOOKERS. The two Indians are Seminoles, older men in town to buy some goods. No one pays them the slightest attention; in fact, they could be invisible. They watch Sonny intently.

ANOTHER ANGLE

Sonny touches his helper's shoulder, motions for him to pay attention. His hands explore the horse's flanks, the neck. He gently rolls back the eyelids for a look, then raises a lip to check his gums, all the while murmuring to his helper, teaching him:

SONNY
(not too much above a whisper)
See? Notice the ribs, how strong he is ... and his teeth look good. And always look into a horse's eyes. Sometimes you can see what they're made of. This is a fine animal ...

ROYCE (O.S.)
Maybe he don't want the buyer to see what kind of blood's runnin' in that Cayuse's veins.

THE TWO INDIANS

Their eyes widen when they hear this. One nudges the other and they peer in between the railings for a better look.

64

FAVORING ROYCE—THE INDIANS POV

Now a tense silence falls over this corner of the stock arena. Royce, very carefully, eases himself down from his perch on the railing, then leans back against it and folds his arms.

ROYCE (cont'd)

But if a horse has got bad blood, there ain't no way it can be covered up.

COWBOY #1

Could be it ain't a horse, either, Royce. Maybe it's a mule.

There is a chorus of laughter following this remark. Sonny's eyes are half-closed and he somehow has made his whole body go completely lax. He's almost somnolent.

THE TWO OLD INDIANS

Watch Sonny carefully, as—

ROYCE

—is beginning to get a little irritated that he's not getting a rise out of Sonny.

THE AUCTIONEER (O.S.)

Numbers ten through fourteen over here at the

registration table! Y'all come on, boys! We got bidness to do!

Royce starts walking toward Sonny, who has now slipped a halter on the horse, getting ready to move out.

ROYCE
(continuing, a loud voice)
A bad blood horse cain't be trusted around other horses, you cain't trust 'em with the boss's equipment, you damn sure cain't turn your back on 'em!

Now he closes in on Sonny, thrusting his face close to his, everyone else out of earshot now . . .

ROYCE (cont'd)
(very low)
Don't think I don't know what you're up to, boy. And don't think the Captain don't know neither. You're playin' a losin' game, mixin' with men.

Sonny stares evenly into his eyes.

SONNY
No need to bother with me, then, is there?

And he leads his horse away.

ON THE TWO OLD INDIANS

They smile mysteriously and nod to each other, then suddenly they vanish.

CUT TO:

16 EXT.—A VILLAGE IN MEXICO—DAY

A small band of APACHE INDIANS peer down on the village from behind some huge boulders on a hill above.

POV—THE VILLAGE

A small corn field, a couple of cows and an oxen, a cluster of adobe huts. The villagers are performing various chores.

THE APACHE LEADER

gives the signal to attack and the Indians mount up. Their war cries pierce the air and they swoop down on the village.

THE VILLAGE

MEXICAN MAN

Apaches!

They kill with bows and arrows, knives and rifles. One Indian shoots a cow with arrow after arrow, then savagely butchers the animal while it is still alive. Women scream, children flee.

The killing is savage, complete, performed in a manner that suggests they have no fear of reprisal.

CUT TO:

17 EXT.—THE TOWN OF PIEDRAS NEGRAS, MEXICO—DAY

A dusty rundown village where a lot of border business is taken care of. The characters hanging out on these streets could be up to anything—smuggling, kidnapping, bounty hunting, murder, revolution.

ON JOHN JULY AND COYOTE

As they ride slowly into town, Coyote is dressed in wild Indian garb, with long feathers sticking up out of his headdress and white silk stockings, and carries a keepsake-looking sword. John also is armed, with a huge Bowie-style sheathed knife at his belt. The two comrades look fearless and relaxed, indifferent to the stares from the other denizens of the town.

ANGLE ON A CANTINA

John and Coyote rein in their horses and look longingly at the cantina. They exchange ironic smiles. Coyote licks his lips in an exaggerated manner.

COYOTE
We'll talk better if we have a taste of whisky.

JOHN

This town must have more juzgados than churches, just so the drunks'll have a place to sleep it off. Let's take care of business first.

CUT TO:

18 INT.—A BUREAUCRATIC OFFICIAL'S OFFICE—DAY

JUAN MALDONALDO, Sub-Inspector General for the State of Coahuila, sits behind his desk chewing a soggy cigar. He is the very soul of Mexican bureaucracy. John and Captain Coyote stand in front of his desk.

MALDONALDO

It is most important, gentlemen, for you to know that El Presidente welcomes you and your peoples to Mexico but wishes you to realize that we have no quarrel with the United States. We have plenty of our own here. And he asks that you honor our laws and our customs, the same as you would in the United States.

JOHN

We will honor your country as a land of liberty. We come from a country where there is no liberty for our people.

Maldonaldo blinks rapidly; he did not expect to hear such an articulate reply from a former slave. Coyote looks sidelong at John, then suddenly begins speaking in Creek dialect.

COYOTE
(with subtitles)

This man speaks like a fool. Tell him we have been fighting the United States since before he learned to walk. Why does he think we are in his country? I could cut his heart out so quickly he'd never make a sound.

JOHN

My friend and fellow chieftain, Captain Coyote, says to kindly advise your President that we will not interfere with any troubles among its own people. Even our children will not be allowed to fight with Mexican children. We will take no sides and will honor your laws.

Maldonaldo starts shuffling some papers around on his desk.

MALDONALDO

We are going to provide for you temporary permits to live along the Rio Grande, until a deed to the land in Nacimiento consisting of fifteen hundred hectares is officially approved in Mexico City—

JOHN

—but how long will this take?

MALDONALDO

It is hard to say, Señor.

John and Coyote look at each other—two veteran negotiators who have begun to smell a rat.

MALDONALDO (cont'd)

In the meantime, while you are waiting for the land to be approved, you will take up camp at El Moral. From this location we would like you to offer your assistance to the government of Mexico.

COYOTE
(low, in dialect)

Here it comes . . .

JOHN

And what is it that you would have us do?

MALDONALDO

El Presidente has heard that the Seminoles are great warriors. He is asking them to help Mexico in fighting the Mescalero and Lipan Apaches and the Comanches who prey upon our citizens along the border, so far from our capital.

JOHN

(to Coyote, in subtitles)

They want us to do their dirty work.

COYOTE

(in subtitles)

Then we will need tools—and more land! And tell him we will take no scalps! No scalps!

John nods, pretends to think over the deal by strolling about the room. Maldonaldo, meanwhile, strikes a chauvinistic give-them-an-inch-they-take-a-mile pose.

JOHN

Advise your President that we accept his offer provided he will double the hectares to be granted us. Tell him also that we will take no scalps.

MALDONALDO

(bristling)

Let me remind you that Mexico is providing you and your people with protection from your enemies, Señor. You do not make the demands.

JOHN

Mexico has spread out its arms to us. But our blood will soon be spilled on Mexican soil. Then we become a part of your country.

MALDONALDO

(a beat)

Very well, I will send your request to Mexico City. But we expect you to engage the hostiles very soon.

JOHN

We will ride against *los indios barbaros.* But first we plant corn. And surely you can spare some oxen—

COYOTE

(nudges him with an elbow)

—and an armorer—

JOHN

—and perhaps an armorer, what we call a blacksmith, to make tools and weapons, also—

Maldonaldo waves in agreement, anything to get them out of the office.

MALDONALDO

Make a list. You'll get what you need.

19 INT.—THE CANTINA NEXT DOOR—DAY

A rough bucket-of-blood joint with a dirt floor and a very low ceiling. A good crowd is on hand, including two AMERICAN

SURVEYORS, distinguished by their khaki outfits with broad suspenders and floppy hats, some Mexican soldiers, a few of their countrymen in sombreros, and some other shady characters. None of these people are used to seeing a black man and a full-blooded Creek Indian in outlandish garb nonchalantly belting back shots of tequila in their saloon.

ANOTHER ANGLE—JOHN AND COYOTE

Suddenly Coyote turns toward the crowd, raises his glass and makes a strange guttural sound from deep in his throat.

COYOTE

Hough!!

An immediate silence falls over the cantina. Then one of the American surveyors roars with laughter and turns to his partner.

SURVEYOR #1

The Injun thinks he's sayin' "bottoms up!"

ON JOHN AND COYOTE

Coyote can't figure out why his toast has not been accepted. John stares at him quizzically.

JOHN

What did you think you were saying?

COYOTE

In Florida once a soldier told me to say such a
word. He say it means Howdy.

JOHN
(smiling)

Try it again.

This time Coyote gives it more flourish and even more volume.

COYOTE

Ho-UYGHH!!!

*There is an outburst of appreciative laughter and the Mexican
contingent hoists their glasses.*

A CHORUS OF VOICES

Ho-UYGHH!

*The cantina suddenly erupts with infectious spirit. Everyone
joins in—except for the two American surveyors.*

ON THE SURVEYORS

*One of the two, whose name is STEVENS, stares intently at
John—and that long Bowie knife.*

STEVENS

That big darky is supposed to be pickin' cotton in

Texas, not traipsin' around down here, drinkin' in a white man's bar.

HIS PARTNER

We're in Mexico now, not Georgia. And in case you didn't notice, white folks is in the distinct minority here.

STEVENS

It's got nothin' to do with where I'm from, goddamnit. That negro is some man's property.

HIS PARTNER

Wouldn't be too sure of that. He might just be one of them black Seminoles that's been driftin' west. They're different—

STEVENS
(interrupting)

—what's that got to do with anything? Slavery is still legal in the Confederacy, and it's legal in Texas.

HIS PARTNER

—one of them runaways that made it into the swamps in Florida. Some intermarried with the Creeks. That'n no doubt has Indian blood in him. 'Bout drove Andy Jackson crazy down there.

They never did surrender.

Stevens thinks about this as he continues measuring John. He gets up, and moves slowly toward the bar. He taps John on the shoulder.

STEVENS
(to John)
Mind if I ask you a question?

JOHN
(most cordially)
Certainly not.

The room goes quiet. One of the Mexicans with the bandoliers nudges his drinking partner and grins.

STEVENS
Are you a cotton-pickin' nigger or a half-breed Indian?

On this Captain Coyote is suddenly all business. With one hand on the handle of his sword, he faces the room, eyeballing the number of potential adversaries they might have to face in a showdown. John doesn't move a muscle or show the slightest sign of fear or tension.

JOHN
I am neither. I am a black Seminole.

STEVENS

You smell like a nigger to me.

Out comes Coyote's antique sword. It makes a rusty, screeching sound as it exits the scabbard; it may be the first time it's ever been drawn. There are a number of men packing sidearms in the cantina but this sword really gets their attention.

JOHN

Mister, your nose betrays you. What you smell is the rotting of your own brain.

John sidesteps Stevens's first punch, spins him around, and with one swift move takes out his Bowie knife and neatly cuts the man's suspenders across the back.

ANOTHER ANGLE

The surveyor turns and tries to throw another punch but it's too late—his trousers slide down around his ankles and he pitches forward awkwardly onto the floor. There is a brief SILENCE, followed by a thunderclap of stupefied laughter.

ON COYOTE AND JOHN

—looking at each other; neither is laughing. John nods, Coyote puts away his sword, they slug back their drinks and walk out of the cantina as the humiliated surveyor struggles to get to his feet.

CUT TO:

20 EXT.—SEMINOLE ENCAMPMENT AT EL MORAL—DAY

VARIOUS ANGLES

—of the Seminoles busy with domestic activities on a wretched plot of desert given them by the Mexican authorities. They have a plow and an ox, and are building, digging, planting corn, etc. A tiny stream flows just past the campground.

ON JOHN JULY AND CAPTAIN COYOTE

—watching everything from a vantage point above the encampment. The plow sends up great clouds of dust from the arid soil.

COYOTE

Can we grow corn in such ground?

JOHN

Would you rather be back in the Everglades?

Coyote grunts.

JOHN (cont'd)

Nacimiento is in a valley where three rivers come together. There is tall grass and good protection from the hostiles.

COYOTE

How far?

JOHN

Two days ride. I want you to see it.

COYOTE

I have already seen it with your eyes.

JOHN

It will make a good homeland.

COYOTE

Then we will get it. But first we have to figure out how these Mexicans think.

CUT TO:

21 EXT.—THE DESERT—DAY

Coyote and a party of TEN SEMINOLES are following tracks. Some are on foot, their eyes glued to the ground, others ride in meandering ways to either side. They are silent, intensely concentrated. Suddenly Coyote makes a series of rapid hand signals and those on foot mount up and move off in another direction.

EXT.—AN APACHE CAMP—DAY

A hidden sanctuary in a narrow canyon. A small group of APACHES are at rest from a recent raiding party. Their horses are tethered at the far end of the canyon. The scene is peaceful and quiet, just after sundown.

CANYON RIM

—where Coyote and his men are peering down. Coyote makes a sign and—

TWO OF HIS MEN

—using dead-fall tree trunks pry a series of large boulders loose in what becomes a terrific ROCKSLIDE straight down into the Apache encampment. All hell breaks loose below.

ANOTHER ANGLE

Six of Coyote's men meanwhile have moved among the horses and are untethering them as the diversion scheme works to perfection.

ON THE HORSES

—running free—a stampede with all of Coyote's men abroad, completing a stunningly swift raid.

ON THE APACHES

—chasing them for a few yards, then stopping. They look at each other with complete surprise.

CUT TO:

22 EXT.—THE DUPUY RANCH—DAY

Sonny is seen patching a section of barbed-wire fencing. Cass Dupuy rides up and beckons for him. Sonny puts down his tools, walks over to stand alongside Dupuy's horse. Dupuy hands him a slip of paper.

DUPUY

When you finish here go on into town and pick up these supplies. Best take the buckboard to haul that feed.

Sonny looks over the list, nods his assent.

DUPUY (cont'd)

You seen my daughter anywhere?

SONNY

No, sir. But her horse is missin' from the corral.

CUT TO:

23 EXT.—OPEN TEXAS COUNTRY—DAY

Teresa is galloping her horse hell-bent for leather across an expanse of sage-covered rangeland. There is exhilaration in her face, in the sense of freedom she clearly is feeling in a moment of complete privacy.

Suddenly, she halts and looks OFF—and SEES a man in a buckboard in the distance.

She stands up in the stirrups, shades her eyes as she identifies Sonny. She starts to call out his name then changes her mind, as if content to watch him in secrecy.

ON TERESA—CLOSE

Watching him, transfixed. Then:

TERESA
(spurring her horse hard)

Yaa-ahh!!

NEW ANGLE

—as Sonny hears this high-pitched cry and sees her coming, he snaps the reins to move the buckboard faster. Teresa rides up onto the road in front of him and then circles the wagon, grinning but not saying anything. Sonny just stares straight ahead like he hasn't even seen her. Teresa rides up alongside the buckboard, deftly jumps from her horse into the back and ties the horse off. Then she plumps down in the seat beside him.

TERESA (cont'd)

Mornin', stranger. Damn fine weather we're havin', ain't it?

83

SONNY

Yes, ma'am, 'specially for South Texas. You from around here or am I gonna have to chase your tail to hell and gone?

Then they both burst into laughter.

CUT TO:

24 EXT.—EAGLE PASS—DAY

A bustling little town—and much-used route to California during the gold rush—with an array of commercial enterprises. Sonny and Teresa ride down the main street. She points to a COVERED WAGON parked with a sign scrawled across the canvas covering: "CALIFORNIA—HERE WE COME!!"

25 INT.—A GENERAL STORE—DAY

There are FOUR LOCAL WOMEN and a tall, bearded, drooping 49ER gold prospector. The women are browsing, and at the same time studying this soiled, road-weary prospector who is buying some supplies.

THE 49ER

... 'bout as much chewin' tobaccy as you can spare, an' a couple pounds of coffee, long as you're at it.

THE STOREKEEPER

Can't but give you two sacks of chew.... Think
there'll be any gold left time you get to
California?

THE 49ER

Well, sir, you by God have just asked the big
question, no doubt about it. If two sacks'll get me
there, I might have a chance.

*There is a small stack of daily newspapers on the counter-top
and the 49er checks out the front page while his order is being
filled.*

THE 49ER (cont'd)

Damn!

The storekeeper turns and looks at him.

THE 49ER (cont'd)
(still reading)

Damn! Imagine that!

A NEW ANGLE

*The doorbell rings as Sonny and Teresa enter. All eyes are on
them. One of the women, MRS. CONOVER, is stunned to see
them together.*

TERESA

Howdy, Miz Conover. How you doin'?

MRS. CONOVER

Just fine, Teresa, just fine.

She looks at Sonny with apprehension, then exchanges a nervous glance with Shopping Lady #1.

Meanwhile the 49er is paying his bill, apparently still baffled by what he's seen in the paper.

THE 49ER

(mostly to himself)

Ain't no tellin' what some folks'll do.

(to the storekeeper)

Well, I'll skedaddle. Much obliged.

He picks up his goods and starts for the door.

THE STOREKEEPER

Say—there's talk of a big storm comin' up out of Mexico. You might want to bed down here til morning.

The 49er waves and goes out.

THE STOREKEEPER (cont'd)

(to Sonny)

What'll it be?

Sonny hands him the list Dupuy gave him. Teresa browses around, doing her best to avoid any small talk with the local ladies.

CLOSE ON SONNY

As he glances at the NEWSPAPER lying on the counter. Very gradually, a shock of recognition comes over him and he emits a high-pitched yet muffled sound.

ON TERESA

She reacts instinctively and moves to Sonny, who has dropped the paper and taken several steps backward. Teresa snatches the paper and the Camera reads over her shoulder, "HEAD OF FAMED SEMINOLE CHIEFTAIN FOUND IN NEW YORK CITY FIRE."

CLOSE ON THE NEWSPAPER

And we see a large SKETCH of the ghoulish, shrunken head of OSCEOLA, Sonny's father. The paper trembles in Teresa's hands as she reads the article.

ANOTHER ANGLE—ALL

Not one of the customers so much as moves a muscle except the storekeeper, who finishes completing Sonny's order. Teresa, a horrified look on her face, puts the paper back on the countertop and stares them all down. Finally:

THE STOREKEEPER (cont'd)
(looking straight at Sonny)
That'll be four dollars and seventy-two cents,
Sonny. You want it on Mr. Dupuy's bill?

Sonny whips out his knife and plunges it violently into the discarded newspaper, pinning it to the countertop.

ANOTHER ANGLE

And all eyes on it, the blade still quivering directly above the headline: "OSCEOLA."

CUT TO:

26 EXT.—OUTSKIRTS OF EAGLE PASS—DAY

A distraught Teresa has the reins to the buckboard and she's driving it hard enough that her own horse, hitched to the back, has to canter to keep up. Sonny sits beside her, bent over with his head in his hands.

CUT TO:

27 EXT.—AN ABANDONED ARMY FORT—DAY

Powerful winds bear down across the desert. A dust storm is in the making.

Teresa whips the buckboard into the fort, startling two wild burros who are browsing around near one of the rundown buildings. Sonny immediately jumps out and starts walking in circles, first one way, then another, obviously trying to get his emotions under control. But he keeps clutching his head as if in pain and Teresa doesn't know what to do, still holding the reins in her hands and watching him. The wind begins to howl; clouds of dust sweep down upon them.

TERESA

Sonny—! Oh, Sonny, goddamnit!

SONNY

Tell me what it said! Every word.

Teresa jumps out of the buckboard, runs to him.

TERESA

Sonny, what do you mean? I don't—

SONNY

—I can't read!

TERESA

What—?

She tries to put her arms around him but he shakes her off.

SONNY

Never mind. Tell me!

It starts to rain. Teresa gestures toward the empty building but Sonny stops her.

SONNY (cont'd)

Now!

TERESA

It—it said the doctor who was at your father's bedside when he died cut off his head and kept it for a souvenir. He would hang it on his children's bedpost when he wanted to punish them.

And here Teresa imagines she sees the scene, as we

FLASHCUT TO:

INT.—A BOY'S BEDROOM—NIGHT

A SIX-YEAR-OLD BOY, speechless with fright, screams sound-lessly as he sees the shrunken HEAD OF OSCEOLA impaled on the post of his bed.

BACK TO SCENE

Tears stream down Teresa's face as she looks at Sonny.

TERESA (cont'd)

Later this doctor gave it to a friend of his who lived in New York. His house burned down a few days ago, and they found ... the head ... in the remains of the fire.

SONNY

I was at his bedside when he died, at Ft. Moultrie, in South Carolina. I was three years old. All these years, Teresa, I thought he had an honorable burial—

The storm now begins to rage, bringing torrents of rain.

SONNY (cont'd)

(shouting above the storm)

—What kind of man would do that? Ain't they done enough to us? They even want to keep parts of our bodies as keepsakes to scare their own children?

He throws his head back and lets out a terrible cry.

SONNY (cont'd)

Who are you people!!?

CODA

Souvenir of Evil

I recently viewed an exhibit on the history of tattoos at a small museum in Flims, a village in the Swiss Alps. The first two floors housed predictable displays of photographs of a variety of body decoration, from tattooing to piercing, along with video monitors featuring practitioners of these arts expounding on method, motive and desire. The third floor contained similar displays, but one area was partitioned off, dimly lit with a separate doorway. In this room was a lamp covered by a shade made out of human skin. The skin, prior to having been flayed, I presume, had been tattooed with the words "Santa Maria," and an illustration of a girl's face. A card explained that this item was created during the 1930s and '40s in Germany. It was on loan from a private collection in the United States.

Of course I had heard about the Nazis making lampshades from the skin of Jews and others they had murdered in their concentration camps, but I had never before seen the evidence, nor had I ever expected to. I was with two friends, the Swiss film and opera director Daniel Schmid, and his assistant, Christophe. The three of us were the only ones present in this section of the museum, and each of us was shocked and horrified in ways we had difficulty describing. Daniel, who had read about the exhibit in a local newspaper, said that no mention of this particular object had been made in the article. Christophe, who is in his early twenties, asked me if I thought it appropriate that such a horror be displayed for the public. I couldn't answer. He suggested that if this were done in America protesters would demonstrate in front of the building. I thought there should perhaps be a warning sign outside this small room apprising people of what they would witness inside, a souvenir of evil.

Before leaving the building, I mentioned to the middle-aged Swiss woman stationed at the entrance desk that I thought some museumgoers might find offensive the display of a lampshade made out of human skin, let alone skin taken from concentration camp victims. She expressed surprise at my remark. "Why should anyone be offended?" she replied. "It's part of the history of this subject."

After I returned to California, where I live, I related to my friend Ira, a former Israeli commando, what I had seen. He told me he thought it was good to have such a thing available for public consumption, so that people would be reminded of The Holocaust, especially in light of ongoing strife in the Middle East. Then Ira told me the following joke.

Bush, Sharon, and Putin meet to discuss the conflict between the Jews and the Arabs in an effort to resolve the problem, but they can find no way to alleviate the crisis. God appears and tells them he's disgusted with the whole thing. He has decided to destroy mankind and take a break. Maybe, He says, in the future, He'll take another crack at it and start again. Then, God disappears.

Bush goes back to the United States and addresses the people. He tells them he has good news and bad news. The good news is that there is a God; the bad news is that He is going to destroy mankind. Putin goes back to Russia and tells his people that he has bad news and terrible news. The bad news is that there is a God; and the terrible news is that He is going to destroy mankind. Sharon goes back to Israel and tells the Israelis that he has good news and wonderful news. The good news is that there is a God; but the wonderful news is that there will never, ever be a state of Palestine.

"That joke could also be told from a Palestinian perspective," I said. "Sure," said Ira, "but it came from the mind of an Israeli."

I thought about the tattooed skin on the lampshade and remembered that, according to Jewish tradition, tattoos were considered taboo. Perhaps the skin was not taken from a Jew (more likely a Gypsy), but of course it doesn't matter. When I was a boy in Chicago, the only people I knew who had tattoos were either sailors or Jewish survivors of concentration camps who had numbers burned into their arms by the Nazis. The Nazis certainly knew of the Jewish prohibition on tattoos. My father, who was Jewish and a rack-eteer, told me never to get a tattoo. If I had one, he said, I could always be identified, and there might come a day when I would prefer not to be. That made sense, so I've never gotten a tattoo.

The more I think about the joke Ira told me, the more I like it. If God destroyed mankind, would it matter? No more than whether the skin on the lampshade was taken from a Jew, because nobody would be around to even consider the question. Another thought: A tattoo is really like a one-eyed jack—even if you peel it off, the other side remains unre-vealed. There's always more to the story.

ONE-EYED JACKS

THE CAST

Rio	MARLON BRANDO
Dad Longworth	KARL MALDEN
Louisa	PINA PELLICER
Maria	KATY JURADO
Bob Amory	BEN JOHNSON
Lon	SLIM PICKENS
Modesto	LARRY DURAN
Harvey	SAM GILMAN
Howard Tetley	TIMOTHY CAREY
Redhead	MIRIAM COLON
Bank Teller	ELISHA COOK
Leader of the Rurales	RUDOLPH ACOSTA
Bartender	RAY TEAL
Bearded Townsman	JOHN DIERKES
Flamenco Dancer	MARGARITA CORDOVA
Doc	HANK WORDEN
Margarita	MINA MARTINEZ

A Paramount Release—A Pennebaker Production—
Photographed in VistaVision—
Colour by Technicolor—
Running Time: 2 hours and 21 minutes

Bibliography

The Authentic Death of Hendry Jones, by Charles Neider (New York: Crest Books, 1960).

Brando: Songs My Mother Taught Me, by Marlon Brando with Robert Lindsey (New York: Random House, 1994).

The Cantos of Ezra Pound (New York: New Directions, 1970).

The Complete Kubrick, edited by David Hughes (London: Virgin Publishing Ltd, 2000).

If They Move ... Kill 'Em: The Life and Times of Sam Peckinpah, by David Weddle (New York: Grove Press, 1994).

The Lost Childhood and Other Essays, by Graham Greene (Middlesex, England: Penguin Books, 1951).

The Mexican Cinema, by Beatriz Reyes Nevares (Albuquerque: University of New Mexico Press, 1976).

Now Dig This: The Unspeakable Writings of Terry Southern 1950–1995 (New York: Grove Press, 2001).

One-Eyed Jacks: The Authentic Death of Hendry Jones, a Screenplay by Sam Peckinpah, November 11, 1957. Revised May 6, 1959.

Sam Peckinpah: The Western Films/A Reconsideration, by Paul Seydor (Urbana and Chicago: University of Illinois Press, 1997).

Barry Gifford's novels have been translated into twenty-three languages. He has received awards for his work from PEN, the National Endowment for the Arts, the American Library Association, and the Writers Guild of America. The screen adaptation of Gifford's novel *Wild at Heart*, directed by David Lynch, won the Palme d'Or at the Cannes Film Festival in 1990. Gifford co-wrote the film *Lost Highway* with Lynch in 1997; the screenplay of *Perdita Durango,* based on his own novel, also in 1997; and the screenplay of *City of Ghosts* with Matt Dillon in 2003.

The author's recent books include *The Phantom Father*, named a *New York Times* Notable Book of the Year; *Wyoming*, named a Los Angeles Times Novel of the Year, which has been adapted for the stage and film; *American Falls: The Collected Short Stories;* and *The Rooster Trapped in the Reptile Room: A Barry Gifford Reader*. His writings have appeared in many publications including *Esquire*, *Rolling Stone*, and the *New York Times*. He lives in the San Francisco Bay Area.

For more information please visit www.barrygifford.com.